ROCKFORD PUBLIC LIBRARY

3 1112 021897984

D1224787

J 398.20932 DICKMANN
Dickmann, Nancy
Egyptian

010620

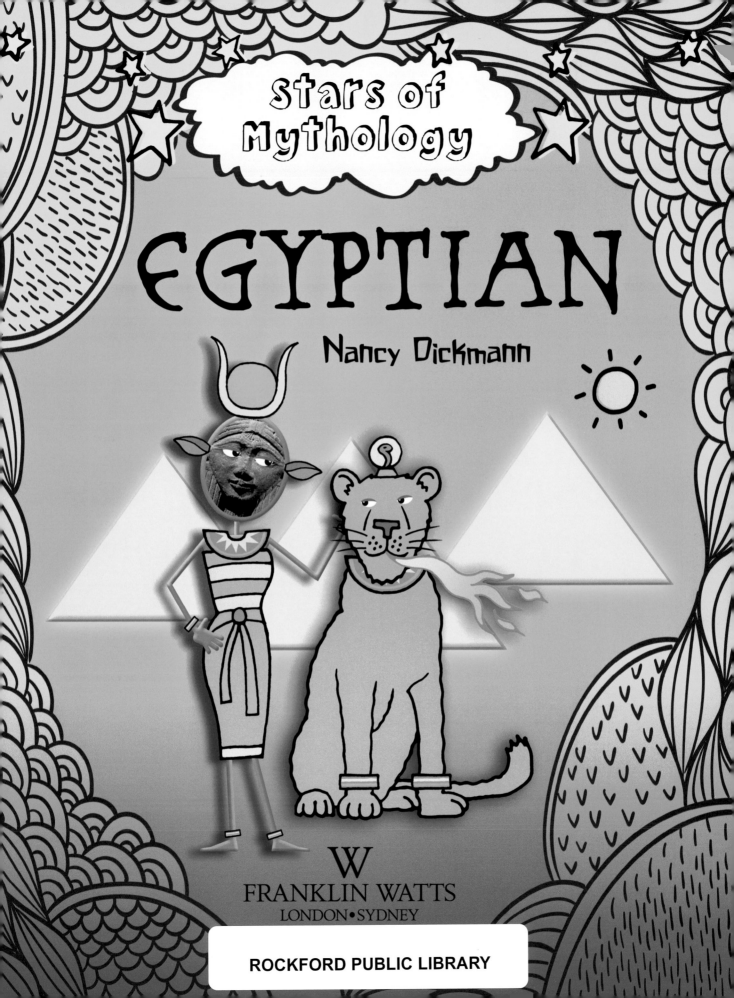

Stars of Mythology

EGYPTIAN

Nancy Dickmann

W
FRANKLIN WATTS
LONDON · SYDNEY

ROCKFORD PUBLIC LIBRARY

Franklin Watts

First published in Great Britain in 2017
by The Watts Publishing Group

Copyright © The Watts Publishing Group, 2017

All rights reserved.

Credits
Series editor: Sarah Peutrill
Series design and illustrations: Matt Lilly
Cover design: Cathryn Gilbert
Picture researcher: Diana Morris

Picture credits: Andrewro/Dreamstime: 6bg. Artosan/
Dreamstime: 17t bg. Denis Burdin/Shutterstock: 23 bg,
25br. Orthan Cam/Shutterstock: 4-5 bg, 26t bg. De
Agostini/Getty Images: 14c, 16cl, 17bl. Diegophoto/
Dreamstime: 15 bg. Mark Eaton/Dreamstime: 27cl,
28tr, 29cl. Evgeniy Fesenko/Dreamstime: 11 bg, 16c
bg. Werner Forman Archive/Alamy: 26c bg, 28tl, 28br,
29cr.http://www.freepik.com">Designed by Freepik:
front cover bg, 1 bg. Hemis/Alamy: 10 bg. Peter Horee/
Alamy: 1cl, 22c, 24tr. Interfoto/Alamy: 15c, 21tc,
21c, 21bcl, 21bc, 31t. Mary Jeliffe/AAA Collection/
Alamy: 4c, 10cl, 12c, 27br. Martina_L/Shutterstock:
front cover cr, 6c, 8c. mountainpix/Shutterstock: 2r, 3r,
22 bg. Nomad_Soul/Shutterstock: front cover cl, 11c,
13tl, 16cr, 24tl, 25tl, 32c. Odyssei/Dreamstime: 18c,
20tc, 20c, 20bl, 21tl. Jac Ravensbergen/Dreamstime:
9t bg. Jose I Soto/Dreamstime: 5t, 5c, 27t. suronin/
Shutterstock: 28cr. UIG/Getty Images: 7c, 9tr.
Utopia_88/Shutterstock: 17br. Waj/Shutterstock: 29tr.
CC Wikimedia: 3bl, 19c, 20tl, 20cr, 20br, 21tr, 21cr,
21bl, 21br, 28cl, 28bc, 29tl, 29br. wrangle/Dreamstime:
17bc, bg. Every attempt has been made to clear copyright.
Should there be any inadvertent omission please apply to
the publisher for rectification.

HB ISBN: 978 1 4451 5190 8
PB ISBN: 978 1 4451 5191 5

Printed in China

Franklin Watts
An imprint of
Hachette Children's Group
Part of The Watts Publishing Group
Carmelite House
50 Victoria Embankment
London EC4Y 0DZ

An Hachette UK Company
www.hachette.co.uk
www.franklinwatts.co.uk

Contents

Egyptian mythology | 4

Osiris and Set | 6
    Sibling rivalry (Set's diary) | 8

Isis and Ra | 10
    Ra's secret name ... revealed? | 12

Tefnut and Thoth | 14
    Tefnut's tantrum | 16

Anubis and Ammut | 18
    Welcome to the underworld | 20

Hathor and Sekhmet | 22
    The sun god speaks | 24

Thutmose and Horus | 26
    The prince's dream (a worker's tale) | 28

Glossary | 30
Further information | 31
Index | 32

Egyptian mythology

Thousands of years ago, people settled along the banks of the River Nile in northeast Africa. The Egyptian rulers (pharaohs) fought wars against their enemies and gave orders for grand temples, palaces and pyramids to be built while ordinary people farmed and built houses. Everyone worshipped many different gods and goddesses who could heal the sick, bring wealth or guarantee a safe birth. Religious beliefs governed all areas of Egyptians' lives. They told myths about their gods and goddesses that attempted to explain how the world came to be, and why things were the way they were.

Gods and goddesses

Egyptian gods and goddesses were seen as magical beings, very different from humans. They often represented ideas, such as justice, or things in the natural world, such as clay, moisture, or the sun. Ra was the sun god and Egyptians believed he was the sun itself. Over time, people told different versions of the stories as their beliefs changed and developed. Sometimes two or more gods or goddesses could overlap, or could be seen as different aspects of the same being.

Many Egyptian structures, such as the pyramids and the Sphinx, are still standing.

Animal heads

In Egyptian art, many of the gods and goddesses were shown with an animal's head on a human body. Sometimes their whole body was that of an animal, such as a baboon or a lion. The Egyptians probably didn't think that the gods actually looked like that. Instead, the animal features were a symbol of the god's personality or role. So for example, Sekhmet has a lion's head to show that she is fierce, and Anubis has a jackal's head because he was a god of the dead, and jackals were often seen around cemeteries.

Gods with animal heads are often shown in tomb paintings.

How do we know?

The Egyptians invented one of the earliest systems of writing. It uses picture symbols called hieroglyphs to represent sounds or words. Hieroglyphic writing was sometimes carved into stone, or written with ink on an early form of paper called papyrus. Many of these writings have survived, and scholars finally figured out how to read the hieroglyphs in 1822. As a result, we know a lot about what the Egyptians thought and believed.

Osiris and Set

Read their story on pages 8–9.

☀ Fact file: Osiris

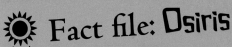

Osiris was one of the most important gods in ancient Egypt. He was born soon after the creation of the world, and he was known as god of the dead and the afterlife as well as a god of fertility. He also gave laws and culture to the people (mortals) on earth.

Osiris was fair and generous, and because he gave life he was loved by the ancient Egyptians. Like many of the Egyptian pharaohs, he married his sister, Isis. Isis was clever and beautiful, and they made a good team.

Osiris in his own words:

Everybody loves me:
The mortals owe me for pretty much everything. I gave them laws and taught them how to farm, and I help their crops grow. What's not to like?

My family:
My father is the earth and my mother is the sky. Literally! Which makes it hard to get us all around the dinner table sometimes.

It's not easy being green:
Laugh if you must, but my green skin shows that I'm all about fertility and rebirth.

Can't live without:
My sister Isis. I mean, my wife Isis. (It's complicated.)

Fact file: Set (also known as Seth)

Set was the younger brother of Osiris, but they were complete opposites. While Osiris was a peaceful, generous god, Set was the god of war, chaos and storms. He was always out to cause mayhem in any way that he could.

For all his mischief, Set was sometimes useful. Every night, as Ra the sun god travelled through the underworld, the giant serpent Apophis tried to destroy him. Set often travelled with Ra as a bodyguard, ensuring that the sun would rise each morning.

Set in his own words:

Trouble and strife:
My wife Nephthys (who's also my sister, naturally) is the goddess of the dead, so it sometimes gets a bit gloomy at our house.

Doing my own thing:
Nobody else looks quite like me. In fact, nobody can agree on what animal I look most like!

Don't talk to me about:
I've had it up to here with people going on about how great Osiris is.

Sibling rivalry (Set's diary)

7TH DAY OF AKHET✲:

Over and over I fight that enormous serpent to make sure that the sun rises, but do I get any credit? No! Instead, I have to listen to everyone telling me how wonderful my brother is. If only I could get rid of him ... but how?

Me first! Me first!

10TH DAY OF AKHET:

I've had a brilliant idea! Now I just need to find some wood and my tools.

20TH DAY OF AKHET:

Well, that went well! Osiris and Isis accepted my invitation to a banquet. I laid on flowers, bread, beer – the works. Then I brought out the wooden box I had built. It was beautiful – gold and blue all over, and Osiris couldn't take his eyes off it. So I suggested that everyone try lying in it, and the one who fit best could take it home. That idiot Osiris jumped straight in, and I was prepared. Before anyone could react, I slammed the lid shut, nailed it tight, and threw it in the river. Job done!

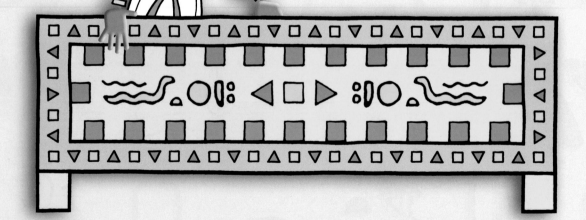

12TH DAY OF PERET:

I can't believe it! Isis has been searching all over, and she's finally found the box. She's going to bring Osiris's body back to Egypt. I wonder if her magical powers are strong enough to bring him back to life? Can't let *that* happen.

16TH DAY OF PERET:

Right, that's done. I managed to find the box and cut Osiris's body into tiny pieces. If I scatter them all across the country, Isis will never be able to revive him.

24TH DAY OF PERET:

That woman just doesn't give up! She even roped in my wife to help her find the pieces. Last I saw they had put him back together and were wrapping him up in bandages. I don't know what good they think that will do! He's obviously dead.

27TH DAY OF PERET:

I don't know how, but Isis managed to bring Osiris at least partially back to life. He's gone down to the underworld to be ruler there, but guess who gets to take over among the living? Not me! I just can't win.

✿ A note on dates: the Egyptians divided the year into three seasons, based on the farming year: Akhet (flooding), Peret (growing) and Shemu (harvest).

Isis and Ra

Read their story on pages 12–13.

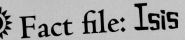

☀ Fact file: Isis

Isis, ike Osiris and Set (see pages 6–9), was one of the five children of Geb (the earth) and Nut (the sky). She married her brother, Osiris, and worked tirelessly to bring him back after their brother Set murdered him. When their son, Horus, was born, Isis was worried that Set would try to kill him too, so she raised him in secret.

Isis was known for her wisdom and clear thinking. She had strong magical powers, but she mainly used them for good, protecting and healing others. She was admired for being the ideal wife and mother.

Isis in her own words:

Current location:
Classified. After what Set did to my husband, I'm not taking any chances. Horus and I are somewhere safe, and that's all you need to know.

If I could have anything:
I'd have Osiris back with me. I've never loved anyone the way I loved him, and I miss him terribly.

I'm known for:
Not doing things by halves. After Osiris died, I cried so much that my tears flooded the Nile. But that helped the farmers, and now they worship me even more than before!

Fact file: Ra

Ra was the first and most important of the Egyptian gods and was associated with the sun. In fact, the sun was so important that there were several gods for it: Khepri was the morning sun and Atum was the evening sun. They may have all been different aspects of Ra.

Ra was a creator god who called every living thing into being. Everything in creation – even Ra himself – had a secret name! If you could learn a person's secret name, you would have great power over them.

Ra in his own words:

My parents:
Who needs parents? I'm so powerful, I created myself out of nothingness.

Check out my rides:
I've got these two fantastic solar boats. One carries me through the sky each day, and the other takes me through the underworld at night.

Best party trick:
I can take my eye out and send it to do my bidding. Once, my children got lost and I was able to relax at home while my eye did the searching.

Ra's secret name ...
revealed?

Everyone knows that Ra's secret name is the source of his power. That's why no one ever knew what it is — until now.

Rumours are flying that the sun god, Ra, has finally told someone his secret name. It's unclear exactly who he revealed it to, but most sources are pointing the finger at his great-granddaughter, Isis. Isis herself has refused to comment.

One thing that is certain is that Ra was bitten by a snake yesterday morning as he was getting ready to make his daily journey across the sky. One of the palace serving women, who didn't want to give her name, said that she had seen Isis in an empty courtyard earlier that morning, rolling mud into a snake shape. "She's a powerful magician, you know," the servant said. "She could have breathed life into anything she made."

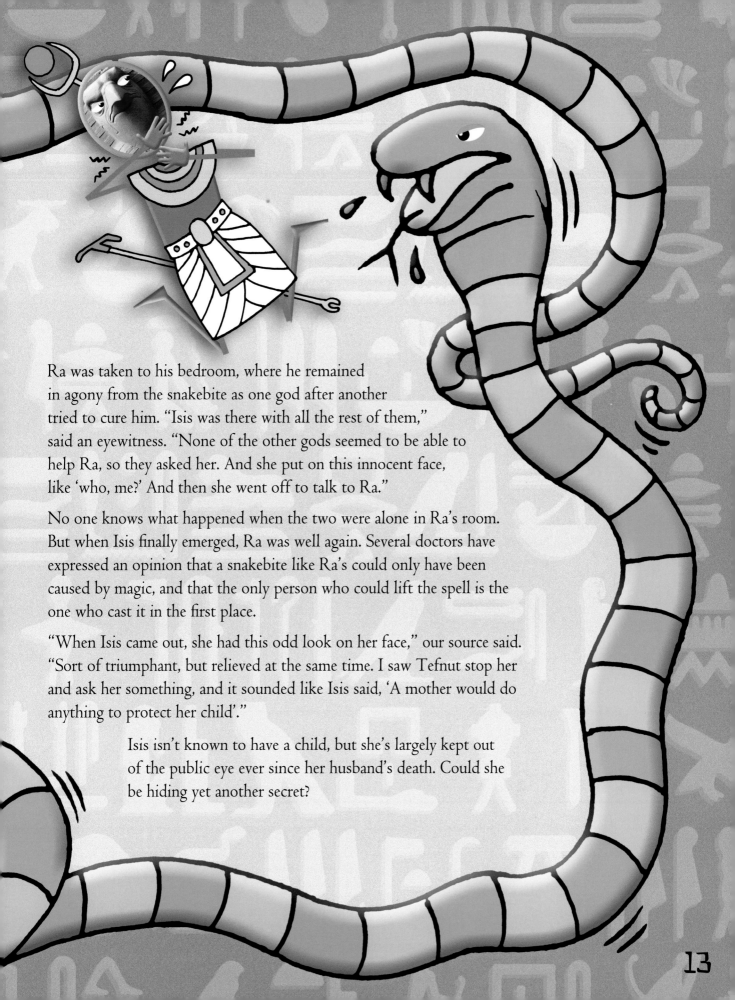

Ra was taken to his bedroom, where he remained in agony from the snakebite as one god after another tried to cure him. "Isis was there with all the rest of them," said an eyewitness. "None of the other gods seemed to be able to help Ra, so they asked her. And she put on this innocent face, like 'who, me?' And then she went off to talk to Ra."

No one knows what happened when the two were alone in Ra's room. But when Isis finally emerged, Ra was well again. Several doctors have expressed an opinion that a snakebite like Ra's could only have been caused by magic, and that the only person who could lift the spell is the one who cast it in the first place.

"When Isis came out, she had this odd look on her face," our source said. "Sort of triumphant, but relieved at the same time. I saw Tefnut stop her and ask her something, and it sounded like Isis said, 'A mother would do anything to protect her child'."

Isis isn't known to have a child, but she's largely kept out of the public eye ever since her husband's death. Could she be hiding yet another secret?

13

Tefnut and Thoth

Read their story on pages 16–17.

☀ Fact file: Tefnut

The goddess **Tefnut** was one of the first beings on earth. Her father, Ra, created himself out of nothingness and then created Tefnut and her twin brother, Shu. Tefnut and Shu later became the parents of Geb and Nut.

Tefnut's name means 'she of moisture', and in a country as hot and dry as Egypt, this made her a very important goddess. She was responsible for bringing moisture, dew and rain to the land.

Tefnut in her own words:

Who's the daddy?:
When my dad, Ra, created me, he was the only living being in the entire universe. So if he wanted children, he had to improvise. He just spat, and suddenly there I was!

Humans owe me everything:
Once when Shu and I were little, we got lost. When we finally got back home, Dad was so happy that he cried, and his tears formed the first humans.

How to keep me happy:
Just give me the respect I deserve. And remember that without the moisture I bring, anyone who displeases me is in for a dry old time.

Fact file: Thoth

Thoth was a powerful god who was associated with all forms of wisdom. He invented hieroglyphs (the Egyptian form of writing – see page 5) and he was in charge of measuring time using the moon. He was also the mediator for disputes between other gods.

Ra, the king of the gods, depended on Thoth for many things. Thoth usually accompanied him as he travelled in his solar boat. He also helped to judge souls in the underworld. Other gods would call on him when they needed help or advice.

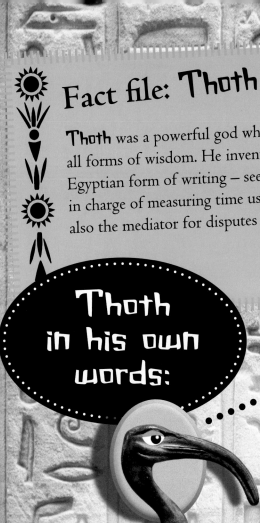

Thoth in his own words:

The original over-achiever:
I invented writing. And the calendar, and science. Astronomy too! Did I mention philosophy? (That was me as well.)

Identity crisis:
Sometimes I'm an ibis, sometimes I'm a baboon. (It's complicated.)

Looking for a good read?:
Check out *Book of the Dead*, my bestseller. Full of information and tips to help you navigate the afterlife.

Crossing boundaries:
My fame has spread so far that they even worship me in Greece.

Tefnut's tantrum

Water's important, right? People need it to drink, to wash, to sail down the Nile — and obviously, to grow their crops. So you'd think that the goddess in charge of water would be first on everyone's list of who to worship, wouldn't you? Well, you'd be wrong.

River Nile

Lake Victoria

Back in the day, people really knew how to worship me. But now they seem more into the younger generation. My grandchildren – like Isis and Osiris – are all that anyone ever talks about. One day I'd had enough, and I went to my father to complain. I thought that he of all people would back me up. But no! He just brushed me off.

As you can imagine, I was furious. So I left, and I took all of the water and moisture with me. We'd see how long people would keep singing hymns to Isis as the rivers dried up!

I got as far as Nubia, but my feet were getting tired, so I changed into a lioness. I could run much faster that way, and I raced all through Nubia, bringing water right and left. But Egypt? That was drying out. Every second without me, it got more and more parched, and the people started to cry out for me.

Well, they had neglected me for years. They could fry for all I cared.

Then one day, just as I was waking up from a lovely nap, I saw a baboon approaching. I recognised him at once: it was Thoth, my dad's right-hand lackey.

"What do you want?" I asked him.

"We want you back," he said. "Egypt needs you, Tefnut."

"They have a funny way of showing it," I told him.

Thoth shrugged. "That's humans for you," he said. "They don't know a good thing when they have it. But now they realise how much they need you."

"And Ra?" I asked.

"Him too. We all want you back, Tefnut. You'll be honoured above all other goddesses. I promise."

Now, I liked the sound of that! I smiled and told Thoth I'd come with him. Everyone deserves a second chance, I guess. But if they ignore me again …

watch out!

You'll be honoured!

Anubis and Ammut

Read their story on pages 20–21.

☀ Fact file: Anubis

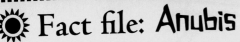

Anubis was usually shown with the head of a jackal. His mother was Nephthys, the wife of Set. However, in many stories his father is actually Set's brother, Osiris. This may be one reason that Set hated Osiris so much.

In the early days, Anubis was the ruler of the underworld, who judged people's souls and decided their fate. Later, Osiris took over these roles, and Anubis became more of a guide, helping dead souls to find their way through the underworld to the afterlife.

Anubis in his own words:

Claim to fame:
When Osiris was killed, I helped Isis to embalm his body. Which means that I invented mummies.
Cool, huh?

Tools of the trade:
I'm never without the scales that I use to weigh a person's soul. If it's any heavier than the feather of truth, then they're in for a bad time.

The original satnav:
Lost in the underworld? Come to me — I know the place like the back of my hand.

Busy, busy, busy:
Not only do I help judge the dead, but I'm also the god of mummification and I help to protect cemeteries. I don't often get a rest!

Fact file: Ammut

Ammut was a fierce creature with the head of a crocodile, the torso of a wild cat and the hind legs of a hippopotamus. She lived in the underworld, and her job was to devour the soul of anyone who was judged to be unworthy of passing into the afterlife.

She was a creature rather than a goddess, and it's not clear where she came from. The ancient Egyptians used her image to ward off evil. It was also a way of reminding themselves to live a good life if they didn't want to be eaten!

Ammut in her own words:

My digs:
I live in the underworld, but it isn't always cold and gloomy. There's a lake of fire that keeps the chill off.

Favourite food:
Souls — as many as I can get!

Pet peeve:
That guidebook Thoth wrote has helped thousands of souls pass the test and be admitted to the afterlife. Which means less for me to eat!

Welcome to the Underworld

Hathor and Sekhmet

Read their story on pages 24–25.

 ## Fact file: Hathor

Hathor was sometimes known as 'the great one of many names', and she was important in nearly every aspect of Egyptian life. She was a goddess of pleasure, beauty, fertility and love, as well as music, the moon and the sky.

Hathor's identity is even more complicated than most of the other Egyptian gods. In some stories she is Ra's mother, and in others she is his wife. She is also sometimes considered to be the mother of Horus, while in other stories it is Isis.

Hathor in her own words:

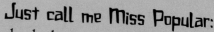

Just call me Miss Popular:
I help the humans with so many things that it's no wonder they love me. Dance, childbirth, even beer – I do it all!

The real me:
I don't even know myself! Sometimes I'm a cow, sometimes I'm a woman and sometimes I'm the eye of Ra.

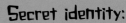

Secret identity:
There are even those who say that Sekhmet and I are different sides of the same goddess. I couldn't possibly comment ... but has anyone ever seen the two of us together?

Fact file: Sekhmet

Sekhmet was a war-like goddess with the head of a lion, sometimes shown as a lioness. In many pictures she wears the sun on her crown. She was often considered to be one of Hathor's different personalities, rather than a completely separate goddess.

Sekhmet was fierce, but she was fair; one of her jobs was protecting Ma'at, the goddess of truth, justice and harmony. She was also a goddess of healing, although she could send plagues against anyone who made her angry.

Sekhmet in her own words:

What's in a name?:
Sekhmet means 'the Powerful One'. Need I say more?

Don't get me angry:
These teeth and claws aren't just for decoration, if you get my meaning.

Favourite colour:
Red.
Which is also the colour of blood. (Coincidence? I think not.)

Deadliest weapon:
Those hot, scorching winds that blow across the desert? That's me. I can even breathe fire.

23

The sun god speaks

Recent weeks have seen the slaughter of thousands of people by the goddess Sekhmet. What caused her uncontrollable rage?

We've been granted an interview with the sun god, Ra, to find out what really happened ...

Ra

Hathor

INTERVIEWER: How did it all begin, then?

RA: Well, not long ago, the humans started disobeying my laws and mocking me. I may be getting on a bit, as you can see, but I'm still the ruler of all creation, so it was bang out of order.

INTERVIEWER: What did you do?

RA: I called my daughter, Hathor – you know that we're so tight that people call her my eye. I knew she'd sort it for me.

INTERVIEWER: And did she?

RA: Yes, but not quite in the way I wanted. When I told her some of the things the humans had been saying about me, she got angry. Really angry. Before I knew it, she had turned into Sekhmet and gone rampaging through the land, killing everyone she met.

Aaaagh!

INTERVIEWER: How did you feel about that?

RA: It seemed a bit over the top, to be honest. And if she kept on killing, soon there would be no one left to worship me! I asked her to stop, but she wouldn't. It was like she was possessed.

INTERVIEWER: Whose idea was the beer?

RA: Mine! It was good, wasn't it? The other gods and I brewed as much beer as we could – thousands of barrels, and as strong as we could make it. Then we dyed it red and added poppy juice to make it even stronger.

Looks like blood!

Slurp! Slurp! Yum!

INTERVIEWER: We've seen pictures of the red beer flooding the fields and valleys. What did Sekhmet do when she found it?

RA: She thought it was blood, so she couldn't resist it! She drank and drank and drank, for a day and a night, and then she passed out.

INTERVIEWER: And the next morning?

RA: When she woke up, she was back to my lovable little Hathor again. It was like none of it had ever happened. But the people will remember … and they won't be so quick to mock me anymore!

Thutmose and Horus

Read their story on pages 28–29.

Fact file: Thutmose IV

Thutmose wasn't a god – he was a real historical figure, a pharaoh who ruled Egypt from around 1400–1390 BCE. Before he became pharaoh, he lived the life of a royal prince, keeping busy with sport and hunting.

Historians think that Thutmose was not the intended heir to the throne. He probably had at least one older brother who should have succeeded their father, Amenhotep II. Thutmose probably stole the crown from his brother and used the story on pages 28–29 to justify his actions.

Thutmose in his own words:

My old man:
He's all right, for a pharaoh. He keeps busy negotiating peace treaties and having temples built, and lets me do my own thing.

How I spend my time:
I help my father out with his military campaigns, but I still have plenty of time to go out hunting in the desert, and to have a snooze from time to time.

I could do without:
Having so many brothers. It really reduces my chances of ever getting the throne myself!

Fact file: Horus

Horus The falcon-headed Horus was an incredibly important god. He was the son of Isis and Osiris, and he fought against Set to avenge his father's murder. Horus represented the ideas of justice, law and order, in battle against Set and the forces of chaos.

In later periods Horus began to merge with Ra, becoming a god of the sky, the earth and even the underworld. For many centuries the Egyptians believed that whoever reigned as pharaoh was the embodiment of Horus on earth.

Horus in his own words:

Look into my eyes:
My right eye is the sun and my left is the moon. During my battles with Set I lost an eye, but Thoth helped to restore it.

Greatest enemy:
My uncle Set. He murdered my father and tried to kill me, too.

Most important job:
I look after each pharaoh to make sure he rules well. And let me tell you, some of them need a lot of supervision.

Anger management issues:
I once cut off my mother's head in a fit of rage. Oops!

27

The prince's dream
(a worker's tale)

Thutmose

Horus

Phew!

I hate sand.

Everywhere you look, that's all you see. Sand on your shovel. Sand in the basket. Sand, sand, sand, stretching all the way to the horizon. It's enough to make a man weep.

A month ago, I was helping to build a temple near the river. It was hard work, but the views were nice, and you occasionally got a cool breeze off the Nile.

But then along came Prince Thutmose.

He commandeered me and a few hundred of the other labourers to come and work on one of his own projects. I'd never seen Thutmose before, but I'd heard a lot of stories about him. He and his brothers all wanted to be the next pharaoh, so they were constantly plotting against each other. Thutmose was just as bad as the rest, but he was young and handsome and you could see him looking good in a crown.

Come with me!

Wow!

It was only when we got to Giza that we found out what the project was.

The three Great Pyramids were shining in the sun – an awesome sight. But Thutmose took us to the place where the giant head of the Sphinx sticks out of the sand.

And then he dropped his bombshell: we were going to dig it out.

The Sphinx

Time to dig!

Honestly, the desert has had centuries to bury that thing. There must be more sand on it than there is water in the Nile!

The prince could tell from our reactions that we didn't fancy the job. So he got all matey and started telling us about this weird dream he'd had.

"I had been out hunting," he told us, "when I stopped to rest under this statue. I fell asleep, and Horus came to me in a dream."

To make a long story short, Horus told Thutmose that if he dug out the statue, he would have his blessing to become pharaoh. Sounds like nonsense to me.

Aaagh!

But a prince is a prince, and ever since then we've been shovelling. My back is sore, my hands are blistered and we haven't even reached the feet yet.

I really, really, really hate sand.

Glossary

afterlife the perfect life that the Egyptians believed a person's soul had after their body had died and travelled through the underworld.

embalm to preserve a dead body or stop it from rotting using special techniques and chemicals.

heir someone who will inherit something. The heir to a throne will be the next person to serve as ruler.

heiroglyph a picture symbol in the Egyptian writing system which can represent a sound or a word.

jackal a type of wild dog found in Africa, which often eats the remains of dead animals.

justice fair, reasonable treatment, also the carrying out of laws in a country.

Ma'at an Egyptian ideal of order, truth and justice. Ma'at could be represented by a goddess of the same name, or by a feather of truth.

mediator a person who attempts to make people who are in conflict agree on a solution.

mortal an ordinary person who will eventually die instead of living forever.

mummy a dead body that has been preserved with special chemicals and wrapped in cloth to prepare it for the afterlife.

myth a traditional story that tries to explain why the world is the way that it is, or to recount legendary events.

Nubia in ancient times, the land to the south of Egypt.

papyrus a paper-like material made from the stems of the papyrus plant, a type of rush, which was used for writing on.

pharaoh a ruler in ancient Egypt. Most pharaohs were men, but a few were women.

solar boat in mythology, a boat in which Ra, the sun god, and the sun are believed to travel across the sky.

soul the spirit of a dead person or animal.

sphinx creature in Egyptian mythology with the body of a lion and the head of a human or an animal.

temple building devoted to the worship of one or more gods.

underworld the place where Egyptians believed that souls went after they died, imagined as being a gloomy underground realm. Souls had to travel through the underworld to reach the perfect place, called the afterlife.

ward off prevent something, or someone, causing harm.

Books

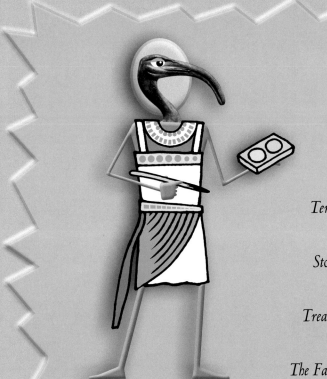

Egyptian Mythology (World of Mythology),
Jim Ollhoff, ADBO & Daughters

Terrible Tales of Ancient Egypt (Monstrous Myths),
Clare Hibbert, Franklin Watts

Stories from Ancient Egypt, Joyce A. Tyldesley,
Oxbow Books

Treasury of Egyptian Mythology, Donna Jo Napoli,
National Geographic Kids

The Fact or Fiction Behind the Egyptians (Truth or Busted),
Kay Barnham, Wayland

Websites

This website from the British Museum has information on Egyptian life, as well as religion:
www.ancientegypt.co.uk/menu.html

Get the low-down on different gods and goddesses on this website:
www.shmoop.com/mythology/#EgyptianGods+Figures

This website has games, puzzles and facts about ancient Egypt:
www.childrensuniversity.manchester.ac.uk/interactives/history/egypt/

Visit this website for an interactive map that tells you all about life in ancient Egypt:
www.dkfindout.com/uk/history/ancient-egypt/

Note to parents and teachers: Every effort has been made by the Publishers to ensure that these websites are suitable for children, that they are of the highest educational value, and that they contain no inappropriate or offensive material. However, because of the nature of the Internet, it is impossible to guarantee that the contents of these sites will not be altered. We strongly advise that Internet access is supervised by a responsible adult.

Index

afterlife 6, 15, 18–19, 21
Amenhotep II 26
Ammut 18–21
Anubis 5, 18–21
Apophis 7, 8

Book of the Dead 15, 19, 20

embalming 18

farming 4, 6, 9, 10, 16
fertility 6
Field of Reeds 21

Geb 6, 10, 14
Giza 29
Great Pyramids 29

Hathor 22–25
heart, weighing of 18, 20–21
hieroglyphs 5, 15
Horus 10, 22, 26–29

Isis 6–13, 16, 18, 22, 27

justice 4, 6, 15, 18, 20, 27

Ma'at 23
mummies 18

Nephthys 7, 18
Nubia 17
Nut 6, 10, 14

Osiris 6–9, 10, 16, 18, 21, 27

palaces 4
pharaohs 4, 6, 26–29
pyramids 4, 29

Ra 4, 7, 10–13, 14, 15, 17, 21, 22, 24–25, 27
River Nile 4, 10, 16, 28–29

Sekhmet 5, 22–25
Set (or Seth) 6–9, 10, 18,27
Shu 14
souls 15, 18–21
Sphinx 4, 29

Tefnut 13, 14–17
temples 4, 26, 28–29
Thoth 14–17, 19, 21, 27
Thutmose IV 26–29

underworld 6, 7, 9, 11, 15, 18–21, 27

wall paintings 5
writing 5, 15

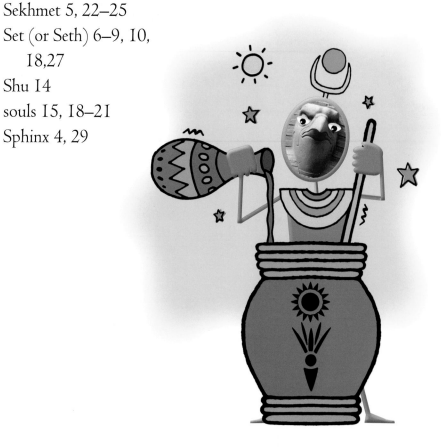

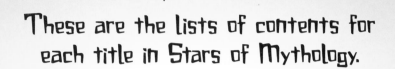

These are the lists of contents for
each title in Stars of Mythology.

Chinese

Chinese mythology

Huangdi and Chiyou • Clash of the gods

Yi and Chang'e • Gone girl

Da Yu and Nujiao • A slight misunderstanding

Gao Xin and Pan Hu • Man's best friend

Zhinu and Niulang • Magpie mystery solved!

Monkey and the jade emperor • The peach thief

Indian

Hindu mythologyy

Krishna and Kamsa • Wrestling for revenge

Savitri and Satyavan • Love conquers all

Rama and Sita • Wedding of the year

Hanuman and Ravana • Monkey mayhem

Parvati and Ganesha • How Ganesha got his head

Hiranyakashyap and Prahlada • Not so immortal after all

Egyptian

Egyptian mythology

Osiris and Set • Sibling tivalry (Set's diary)

Isis and Ra • Ra's secret name ... revealed?

Tefnut and Thoth • Tefnut's tantrum

Anubis and Ammut • Welcome to the underworld

Hathor and Sekhmet • The sun god speaks

Thutmose and Horus • The prince's dream (a worker's tale)

Roman

Roman mythology

Dido and Aeneas • All for love

Romulus and Remus • A shepherd's diary

Juno and Vulcan • The golden throne

Castor and Pollux • Family feud

Hercules and Atlas • Tricked!

Jupiter and Baucis • Unexpected guests

Greek

Greek mythology

Zeus and Europa • Swept away

Perseus and Medusa • Diary of a hero

Theseus and Ariadne • Royally dumped

Hades and Persephone • Phew, what a famine!

Athena and Arachne • War of the weavers

Daedalus and Icarus • Air crash horror

Viking

Norse mythology

Odin and Baugi • A letter to Suttung

Skadi and Njord • Worst day ever

Tyr and Fenrir • When good pets go bad

Thor and Loki • Wedding mayhem

Freyr and Gerd • Playing hard to get

Frigg and Baldur • A mother's love